FashionMuseum
Bath

One of the world's great museum collections of historical and contemporary dress.

BATMC I.10.61
BATMC I. 10.61A
BATMC I. 10. 52
2 PLACE VENDOME
PARIS

THE FASHION MUSEUM

The Fashion Museum is one of the world's great museums of fashionable dress. This illustrated book features some of the treasures from the Museum collection, as presented in the exhibition *A History of Fashion in 100 Objects*, on display in the Fashion Museum Bath.

Taken together, these original historical pieces give a snapshot view of dress history from around 1600 to the present day.

Fashion is about the here and now, but it is also a part of history, whether this is a personal story or a significant moment in world affairs. Each of these featured objects has something important to tell us not only about the history of fashion, but also about how people at the time interpreted and reacted to what was going on in the world around them.

The Fashion Museum came to Bath as the Museum of Costume in 1963 when collector and writer Doris Langley Moore gave her collection of fashionable dress to the city. At that time, Langley Moore estimated that there were 5,000 items in her collection; it took two removal lorries to bring it from storage in London to Bath.

Today, the Fashion Museum houses over 100,000 objects, and is still growing to reflect the ever-evolving world of fashionable dress.

Collection of late nineteenth century shoes belonging to Mary Chamberlain
Gift of the Executors of the Estate of Mary Endicott Chamberlain Carnegie

EARLY FASHIONS

The earliest garments in the museum collection date from the Elizabethan and Jacobean ages. Because textiles are so fragile, these are extremely rare survivals.

Many of these pieces were clearly preserved because they are so exceptionally decorative. Embroidery of this period was highly skilful and England was particularly renowned for the beauty and quality of its needlework. As well as being produced in workshops and guilds, embroidery was undertaken in the home, either by women of the household, copying from pattern books, or by professional itinerant workers hired for their design and needlework skills.

Linen, imported from the Netherlands and Germany, was used for garments worn beneath outer clothes – shirts for a man and shifts for a woman, for example. Sometimes parts of these garments were visible, such as the collar or front opening of a shirt, and these might be just as beautifully decorated as the outer garments, often in a style of embroidery called blackwork, which used black dyed silk thread.

These early fashions were made by hand; they date from a time before garment and textile production was mechanised. The linen and cotton from which the shirt, waistcoat and petticoat were made was woven on hand operated looms. Pattern pieces were cut from the cloth by hand and then embroidered and made up into garments by skilled workers, both men and women. It was a time-consuming business and all the featured pieces you see here would have been costly and therefore precious.

Detail of blackwork embroidery and metal thread lace on tabbed gauntlet cuff of glove, ca.1620s
Courtesy of the Worshipful Company of Glovers of London

1600s A TUDOR MAN OF FASHION

This shirt is the oldest complete garment in the Fashion Museum collection. It is beautifully decorated with hand-embroidered motifs of flowers and insects, probably stitched by a professional embroiderer, working from a design copied from a pattern book.

The shirt would have been worn under a doublet; a short, tight-fitting jacket. Breeches or trousers had not yet been invented: instead the late Elizabethan man of fashion would have tucked his shirt into trunk hose, and worn tube-like canions on his legs. A short cape worn over one shoulder completed the look.

This shirt possibly belonged to Sir Christopher Harris of Devon, who worked for the Royal Navy alongside fellow West countryman Sir Walter Raleigh.

Lent by the Vaughan Family Trust

1610s UNDRESS

This long sleeved garment was called a waistcoat in the 1600s, and was worn with a skirt known as a petticoat or kirtle, with a loose gown over the top. Despite the ornate embroidery, it was made for 'informal' wear. Aristocratic women wore informal dress at home, as the home was also a public space, for receiving visitors.

We think this could have belonged to Lady Alice L'Estrange, the wife of a Member of Parliament during the reign of James I. Records give tantalising glimpses of the couple's frequent trips to London: once, they spent £163 on 'goods' for their home, Hunstanton Hall in Norfolk.

Lent by the Bateman-Porter family

1700s PETTICOAT

Although this looks to our modern eye like a standalone skirt, it was the part of a woman's dress called a petticoat. The main gown or robe was put on over it like a coat and worn open at the front, so the petticoat was very much designed to be seen.

The colourful embroidery includes motifs of flowers, figures and even a ship – a nice symbol of the exchange of ideas and materials that was so crucial in fashion. In Britain, the East India Company received a Royal Charter in 1600 to trade with Asia and India, including a flourishing trade in cotton and silk goods.

Gift of Mrs Hallett

1700 QUALITY NEEDLEWORK

This woman's waistcoat has been embroidered with a design of fanciful birds. The influence of India and China was very important in the 1600s and early 1700s, and the style of embroidery and design motifs show an Eastern sensibility. Needlework was part of a girl's education and considered an appropriate pastime for women of all social classes.

The waistcoat would have been worn under a gown, in non-formal situations, perhaps in the home. The quilting gave some shape and support to the body, so it was a comfortable alternative to the rigid boned stays (the contemporary word for corsets) that were required wear for more public occasions. Non-rigid garments like this were sometimes called jumps.

18TH CENTURY FASHIONS

Fashion was regarded as an essential part of good taste in the 18th century. This was particularly true in France: Louis XIV at the Palace of Versailles cultivated spectacular and glittering courts where the most splendid and up-to-the minute dress was required wear. Largely because of this demand, a fashion industry was well-established in France, with the finest silks in Europe produced in Lyon.

For women, silk was the principal fabric of fashion, until cotton started to become popular around the 1790s. Partly a response to social and political changes – not least the outbreak of the French Revolution in 1789 – a simpler, less ostentatious mood emerged, featuring softer fabrics and lighter colours.

The new mood had an equal impact on men's fashion. The 1700s was the age of the Enlightenment, the philosophical movement that dominated thinking and shaped discussions in coffee houses and discourse in printed pamphlets. As the century went on, and Enlightenment thinking became more mainstream, it found expression, for men, in a more relaxed style of dress. The standard dress for a gentleman was still a coat, breeches and waistcoat, but the silhouette became less stiff, and, instead of full-bottomed wigs, men wore their natural hair.

Embroidered silk coat, breeches and waistcoat, 1770s
Acquired with the assistance of Bath City Corporation

1730s DRESS FOR SOCIABILITY

This open robe was worn with a silk petticoat, which filled the gap at the bottom and was designed to be seen. The gap at the top was filled with a triangular piece of decorative fabric called a stomacher, which had to be pinned to the robe each time it was worn.

The dress provides a picture of what a visitor to Bath might have worn during the city's fashionable heyday. Visitors had been coming to the city since Roman times to take the health-giving waters; but it was in the early 1700s – the time of the great fashion leader Beau Nash – that the city became the resort of choice for 'polite society'.

Gift of Mrs Woolstenholme and the Executors of the Estate of Lorna Lewis

1750s COSTLY LUXURY

Men's fashion in the 1700s was every bit as decorative as women's. This velvet coat, with its big, turned back cuffs and full skirts, was worn with a powdered wig.

Velvet was a luxury cloth, and the height of fashion for menswear in the mid-1700s. Here, the design has been created by cutting a pattern into the pile of the velvet, while leaving the dark red areas smooth. The effect is highly sculptural; when combined with the breeches in the same fabric, it must have been quite dazzling.

Gift of Mrs J K McNair

1760s FRENCH FASHION

With its loose pleats flowing from the shoulders, this style was known as a sack-back or robe à la française. Although it grew out of informal wear, by the 1760s the sack-back was the style of choice for formal occasions. This extravagant example, in saffron yellow silk woven with metal thread, is French fashion at its most opulent.

In France, fashion was regarded as an aspect of the decorative arts. One particularly influential figure in the mid-1700s was Madame de Pompadour, official mistress of Louis XV. She set fashion trends, and entertained leading thinkers of the day in her Paris salon.

Lent by Mrs M E Lloyd

1770s A SOFTER STYLE

Fashion in the first half of the 1700s favoured heavy brocaded silks with strong colours and designs. In the second half of the century – in the years leading up to the French Revolution – a lighter style began to emerge. This sack-back gown is very graceful, with its light colours, lightweight silk and sprigged design.

Gift of Mrs P E Green

1780s MACARONIS

The pink breeches alone would have been enough to make this a star outfit, but it is also interesting because it shows the style of the man's coat evolving. We are no longer seeing big, turned-back cuffs on the sleeves, and full skirts have been replaced by a much narrower silhouette.

Its design may have been influenced by the flamboyant fashions of the Macaronis in the 1770s. Macaronis favoured tight-fitting suits and towering wigs. They were figures of fun, often just returned from the Grand Tour of Italy. Apparently, the name came because they loved everything Italian, including macaroni pasta.

Gift of Mrs K A Freebody

1780s CLOSED GOWN

With the new closed gowns there was no need for a separate stomacher. Here, the lightweight silk, and natural colour palette, illustrate the lighter mood emerging in the second half of the century. The gown is embroidered in tambour stitch, worked with a tambour hook.

The fashion in the 1780s was for large white cotton handkerchiefs worn bunched up in the front over the chest. These were called neckerchiefs or buffons, and, like any new fashion, provoked critical comment at the time: *"Ladies with neckerchiefs puffed up so high their noses were scarcely visible"*.

Gift of Mrs Clease

19TH CENTURY FASHIONS

Fashion in the early 1800s took inspiration from the ancient classical world, fuelled by the archaeological discoveries at Herculaneum and Pompeii. For women, simplicity was key, with white being the colour of choice, and shapes evoking Greek and Roman statuary. The emphasis was on beautiful drapery, natural, flowing lines, purity, and lack of ornament.

A huge change in menswear at the beginning of the 1800s was the move from breeches to trousers. It did not happen overnight, and there was an interim stage of a kind of extended breeches called pantaloons, rather like short leggings. By around 1820, the legs had become longer and looser, like the trousers of today.

The shape of the female silhouette changed repeatedly during the course of the 1800s. By the 1820s, sleeves became fuller, and, instead of the slender column-like forms of the 1810s, the skirts too became more voluminous. Within forty years, this would lead to the enormously wide skirts of the Victorian age.

These changing shapes called for corresponding re-designs of what was worn underneath. Women initially needed layers and layers of petticoats to achieve the fuller skirts that fashion demanded. In the 1850s an iconic new invention was patented – the cage crinoline. The structure was attached to the waistband, and comprised a series of steel hoops joined with tape. The effect was a huge bell-like shape that felt cool and airy to wear. By the 1870s, the shape of the skirt had changed again, with the main bulk at the back; this led to the development of a new garment, commonly known as the bustle. The bustle was a pad, often of horsehair, attached at the back, and supporting the skirt to give that distinctive new silhouette.

Red silk plush dressing gown, 1880s
Gift of Sir James Cory

1800 THE FASHION FOR MUSLIN

By the turn of the century, the shape and design of the gown had altered radically. In this printed evening gown, both skirt and bodice are now closed, so the gown can be put on over the head; the waistline is right up under the bust; and the soft fabric is allowed to fall into a simple column-like shape.

The gown is made of muslin, a lightweight cotton fabric that had originated in India, though by this date it was also produced in Britain. Around 1800, muslin became the fashion fabric of choice, and there was huge demand for its production.

1810s JANE AUSTEN STYLE

White cotton frocks, as they now became known, were wardrobe essentials, but fashion found endless ways to vary the theme. Here, a fleck of red and blue has been woven in, and a triple flounce added to the hem. Long sleeves were fashionable for evening wear at this time, here with a little puff at the top. The effect is very demure and simple.

Jane Austen's *Pride and Prejudice* was first published in 1813, and one can imagine her heroines wearing a frock just like this.

Gift of Miss I K Davies

1830s DANDYISM

This is a rare survival of a complete man's outfit from the period. The narrow-waisted wool coat, worn with trousers and an ornate waistcoat, offers a picture of the last flowering of the dandy. The age of Beau Brummel, with gentlemen of fashion paying extreme attention to the cut of a coat, was a key movement in fashion in the early 1800s and men took great care over the way they looked. This outfit belonged to William Beauclerk, the 9th Duke of Saint Albans. One of his titles was Hereditary Grand Falconer, and he even had his gold buttons decorated with a little hawk.

Gift of Lord Wakehurst

1830s PUFFED SLEEVES

With its crisp pleating at shoulders and cuffs, this lustrous silk gown really makes a feature of its enormous gigot or 'leg of mutton' sleeves. A belt with a jewelled buckle completes the look. Jewellery in the 1830s included long neck chains suspending a watch, eyeglass, or even a scent bottle, which were often tucked into the belt.

This dress is carefully stitched by hand, but the silk fabric from which it was made was most probably woven on a new Jacquard loom. Fashion was becoming increasingly mechanised and the days of hand-loom production were waning.

Gift of Miss L Ewart

1840s THE SEWING MACHINE

The most distinctive thing about this striped wool dress is the row of wonderful blue silk pompoms down the front. They are as irresistible to us now as they must have been to whoever bought the dress in the 1840s.

But the dress also illustrates a fashion revolution. In 1846 Elias Howe patented the sewing machine, and fashion production changed forever. From this time, almost all dresses, including this woven wool gauze dress, were partially machine-made, with some finishing, such as sewing on buttons, done by hand. Fashion just got quicker, meaning too that the pace of change speeded up.

Acquired with the assistance of The Art Fund, MLA/V&A Purchase Grant Fund, Heritage Services Acquisition Fund and a private benefactor

1870s DAY DRESS

A cotton gauze bodice, skirt, overskirt, and belt make up this striking striped day dress. As more manufacturing processes were mechanised, including sewing and cutting, more ornate patterns were possible, leading to more sophisticated seaming and shaping of dresses.

The dress may have been worn with a crinolette to give shape and lift to the back of the skirt. The crinolette was composed of a series of half hoops suspended from a tape around the waist. Some had a system of ties allowing you to adjust the size – so it was an intricate piece of fashion engineering.

Gift of Miss and Mrs Robertson

1880s BUSTLE DRESS

Unfashionable from the mid-1870s, the bustle returned in an exaggerated form in the mid-1880s. Straw-filled cushions and steel hoops made the skirt jut out like a shelf from the small of the back.

This ribbed silk dress, comprising a separate bodice and skirt, is the first of our star objects to carry the maker's name: stamped on the internal belt, or waiststay, in the bodice of the dress, are the words 'Nicholson and Wordley', who were dressmakers in Camden Town, London. It is a key moment in our story and paves the way for the designer fashion of the future.

Gift of C P Clarke

COLLECTION:

LACE AND WHITEWORK

STAR OBJECT:
Collar c. 1827

DESCRIPTION:
Triple layered pelerine with pendant squared ends in front. Cream embroidered net, padded satin stitch trailing leaf and flower design and needle lace fillings.

COLLECTION NOTES:
Lace accessories – collars, cuffs, shawls, stoles, bonnets, veils and caps – were all vital to completing the fashionable look of the day. Whitework – white embroidery on white fabric – was quicker and therefore not as costly to produce as lace, but it was used almost as a lace substitute in the 1700s and 1800s.

Gift of Margaret and Alison Birch

COLLECTION:
STOLES SHAWLS AND SCARVES

STAR OBJECT:
Stole, c. 1812

DESCRIPTION:
Red fancy striped plush, lined with strawberry pink silk. About 0.6 metres wide by 2.4 metres long.

COLLECTION NOTES:
As part of Doris Langley Moore's original collection, this was one of the objects that arrived in Bath packed into a fleet of removal lorries in 1963. It was a particular favourite for Langley Moore; she wrote that this was one of the treasures of her collection that she found hardest to part with.

Gift of F M Moore

COLLECTION STORIES

The Fashion Museum is home to an outstanding collection of historical fashionable dress. Within this Collection are hundreds of fascinating individual fashion stories, a number of which are highlighted in the Collection Stories gallery at the Fashion Museum. You are invited here to look behind the scenes into the museum's 19th century store to uncover some of these hidden narratives.

Collection Stories is a curators' pick of objects in the Museum collection, from shoes and bonnets to lace and wedding dresses. These chosen objects hint at the astonishing size and depth of the collection; but we can also look at them in detail to discover more about the people who wore them, the people who collected them and what they tell us about the history of fashionable dress.

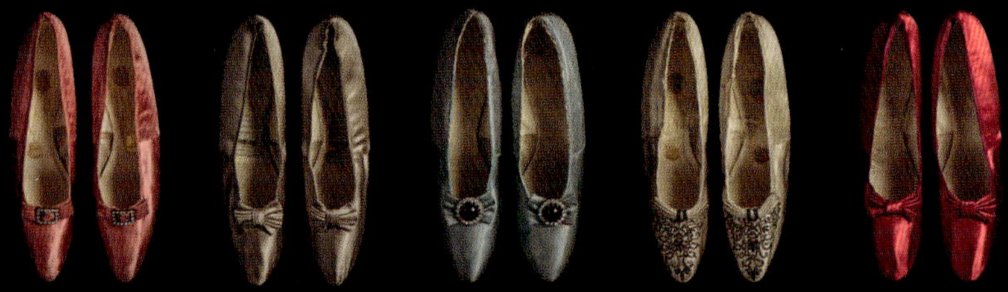

COLLECTION:
WOMEN'S SHOES

STAR OBJECT:
Shoes c. 1898

DESCRIPTION:
Silk satin shoes richly embroidered with glass beads and diamanté. Made by Maxen-Gantiez, 15, Rue de Colisee, Paris,

COLLECTION NOTES:
Part of a large collection of dress belonging to Mary Chamberlain, including a stunning 35 pairs of shoes and boots. American-born Mary Crowinshield Endicott married British politician Joseph Chamberlain in 1888 and travelled to Paris regularly to update her wardrobe.

Gift of the Executors of the Estate of Mary Endicott Chamberlain Carnegie

COLLECTION:
MEN'S WAISTCOATS

STAR OBJECT:
Waistcoat 1850s

DESCRIPTION:
Cream silk with coloured silk embroidery.

COLLECTION NOTES:
Worn to attend court during the time of Queen Victoria. Late 18th century style – knee breeches, waistcoat, tailcoat and silk stockings – was the accepted dress code for gentlemen attending a royal 'drawing room'.

Gift of Rene MacColl

20TH CENTURY FASHIONS

The 20th century was the age of the fashion designer, moving from small dressmaking establishments, frequently never named, to giant global franchises bearing the name of star designers, with celebrity status in their own right.

The increased pace of technological change had a marked effect in fashion throughout the 20th century, with ever new and evolving synthetic fibres and fabrics and production methods giving rise to a sophisticated ready to wear system. Whilst garments were now pre-sized and therefore more affordable, the new fabrics not only looked luxurious but had their own properties – such as give and stretch – that suited them to the changes in men's and women's lifestyles throughout the century.

With the onset of the Second World War in 1939, a mood of austerity prevailed in the fashion world. It was epitomised in Britain by the Make Do and Mend campaign, encouraging people to care for existing clothes and to make new from old, and proving that fashion exists outside the formal commercial systems, and is about the will to be inventive and resourceful in creating personal style.

This mood changed spectacularly in February 1947, when the French designer Christian Dior launched his first collection to international acclaim. It seemed to signal the rebirth of dazzling, headline fashion after the privations of war. The collection – which became known as 'The New Look' – brought out women's natural graces, with full, tulip-like skirts blossoming from slender, stem-like waists.

The final decades of the century were dominated by youth fashion. Spearheaded by young French and British designers, the new fashions included mini-skirts for women and bright colours for men, and were all about freedom and fun.

Black wool jacket and skirt from Christian Dior's 1947 New Look collection
Gift of Dame Margot Fonteyn de Arias / Langley Moore Collection

1908 WEDDING DRESS

This beautifully decorated wedding dress is by one of Britain's first fashion designers – Lucile. Lucile, or Lucy Duff-Gordon, was an acclaimed innovator in the couture world, and also an astute businesswoman: she was among the first to organise fashion shows and train professional models, to name her dresses, and to send fashion drawings of her collection to the press.

She also famously survived the sinking of the *Titanic*, though there was public outrage at the fact that her lifeboat – designed to hold forty people – had left with only ten on board.

Acquisition supported by the Heritage Services Acquisition Fund

1929 TROUSERS FOR WOMEN

Women in trousers is one of the big fashion stories of the twentieth century. As frequently happens in fashion, the new trend emerged from the fringes – in this case, from the more relaxed, informal styles of holiday wear. These beach pyjamas consist of wide, flowing trousers, with matching jacket and top, decorated with Chinese style embroidery. They're among the most important of all our star objects: trousers for women had arrived.

Gift of Mrs Maud Fuller/Langley Moore Collection

1930s HOLLYWOOD GLAMOUR

This gown is by Donguy of Paris but, increasingly, 'Paris look' clothes were available for the mass market. New synthetic fabrics brought dress prices down, giving more and more women the chance to look like their favourite screen goddess.

The artificial silk for this evening gown has been cut on the bias, giving it the classic slinky, clingy silhouette of the 1930s. For men, full evening dress consisted of white tie and tails, as exemplified by legendary Hollywood dancer Fred Astaire in the 1935 film *Top Hat*.

Gift of Josephine Carpenter

1945 VICTORY IN EUROPE

Those who lived through the Second World War in Britain always remember the Blackout. Every evening, all windows had to be covered with blinds made of thick 'blackout' fabric, so the lights would not provide a target for enemy bombers.

Blackout fabric was unrationed and therefore a popular choice for home dressmakers. This dress was made for a party celebrating the end of the war in Europe in 1945. Its broad stripes made of blackout fabric make it a very special memento from the war years.

Gift of Ann King

1950s DIOR STYLE

It could be said that there were two basic fashionable shapes in the 1950s: full, flared skirts and narrow, slender silhouettes. This full-skirted example is by Christian Dior. Throughout the 1950s couturiers in Paris, including Dior, set the trends; here, in an ensemble called *Romanesque* from 1950, he is at his creative peak. The dress achieves elegance through its effortless simplicity – and its exuberant use of fabric. It also pioneers the idea of a shorter skirt even for evening wear.

Gift of Hilary Lyma Murdoch

1968 PEACOCK REVOLUTION

Throughout the 20th century, menswear had tended to be sombre and understated. At the end of the 1960s, all that changed, and men's fashion started looking back to the dazzling ostentation of the past. Restrained suits and ties were replaced with the colourful, the bold and the fancy.

This jacket is by Michael Fish, who opened his iconic boutique Mr Fish in London's Mayfair in 1966. The jacket belonged to the dramatist Noel Coward, towards the end of his life – demonstrating that the new youthful fashions were not just for the young.

Gift of the Executors of the Estate of Sir Noel Coward

1980s ROYAL INFLUENCE

David and Elizabeth Emanuel shot to fame when they designed the dress for Lady Diana Spencer's wedding to Prince Charles in 1981. The dress spawned a thousand copies, becoming the style that summed up the early 1980s. This red ballgown, also by the Emanuels, follows a very similar design: its shape and style was seen at balls and dances up and down the country.

Diana acted as an ambassador for the British fashion industry in the 1980s, in the UK and overseas. She was a fashion trend-setter, with her clothes much copied on the high street.

Gift of Richard Lester

MODERN FASHIONS

The Fashion Museum keeps its modern collection up to date through its unique Dress of the Year scheme.

Each year since 1963 the Museum has asked a leading fashion expert to choose a dress or ensemble to represent the newest and most influential ideas in contemporary fashion. They are free to choose from among the international collections whatever item they find the most exciting, or that best sums up a moment. The selection is donated to the Museum by the designer or maker. The result is an outstanding year by year record of recent fashions.

For our final star objects we've chosen four recent selections from our Dress of the Year Scheme.

Hyper-Cherries headpiece by Piers Atkinson 2008
Gift of Piers Atkinson

2011 SARAH BURTON FOR MCQUEEN

Dress of the Year 2011 was chosen by Hamish Bowles of American *Vogue*, and is by Sarah Burton for Alexander McQueen. Burton's whole collection was white: the story goes that this was to hide the fact that she was also designing the wedding dress worn by HRH The Duchess of Cambridge in April 2011. The dress is simple in essence, but the feathery embroidery and sculptural pleats turn it into something sensational.

Gift of McQueen/Dress of the Year Collection

2012 DIOR DEBUT

Dress of the Year 2012 is from Belgian designer Raf Simons' first collection for Christian Dior, and was chosen by Vanessa Friedman, then fashion editor at the *Financial Times*.

On selecting it, Friedman commented that this 'evolution of a dress' represents the moment 'when a new designer took over at the ultimate couture house'. Simons went back to the archives: he took the idea of a 1950s Dior style, cut it off to tunic length, and teamed it with sharp black trousers to bring it right up to date for today's woman.

Gift of Dior/Dress of the Year Collection

2017 'WE SHOULD ALL BE FEMINISTS'

2017 was the 70th anniversary of Christian Dior's first collection, the iconic New Look, the style that redefined femininity for the post-war age.

Also in 2017, for the first time in its history, the House of Dior was headed by a woman, Maria Grazia Chiuri. Her slogan T-shirt is worn with a black jacket and see-through skirt and was chosen as Dress of the Year by Sarah Bailey, then editor of *Red* magazine.

Chiuri's designs re-interpret some of the signature pieces of the House of Dior to reflect the changing needs of today's women, freed, as she put it, 'from the stereotypical categories of masculine/feminine, young/not so young.'

Gift of Dior/Dress of the Year Collection

WE
SHOUL
ALL B
EMINIS

FASHION AND HISTORY

The Dress of the Year selection for 2018 includes two ensembles, one designed by Nicolas Ghesquière for Louis Vuitton, the other by Kim Jones for Dior.

They were chosen by fashion journalist, author and editor of *AnOther* magazine, Alexander Fury, who wanted to highlight the influence of history on fashion. Ghesquière updates 18th century court clothing by pairing a brocaded frock-coat with running shorts and trainers; Jones looks to Dior's own heritage, taking as inspiration the *Oblique Collection*, from Autumn/Winter 1950, which used bold diagonal lines to wrap the body.

There is also a very contemporary note of gender fluidity. The frock coat is based on historical menswear, translated here into womenswear, while the Dior man's suit refers to an earlier womenswear line. The use of colour – pink for the menswear and blue for the womenswear – is another play on gender stereotypes.

Gift of Dior and Vuitton/Dress of the Year Collection

Blue silk damask shoes with wooden clogs, part of an 18th century set.
Accepted by HM Government in lieu of Inheritance Tax from the estate of Francis Charles Penley and allocated to the Fashion Museum Bath, 2018.

Published in 2019 by Jarrold Publishing in association with Fashion Museum Bath.
01/19-92328 ISBN 978-0-85101-637-5

Design: Jamieson Eley, Jarrold Publishing

www.jarrold-publishing.co.uk

Fashion Museum Bath
Assembly Rooms,
Bennett Street,
Bath BA1 2QH
www.fashionmuseum.co.uk
24 Hour information: +44 (0)1225 477867

The Fashion Museum collection is managed by Bath & North East Somerset Council and is Desginated as a collection of outstanding significance by Arts Council England.

Bath & North East Somerset Council

Designated as an Outstanding Collection D